Tamara DeStefano

Dancing Barefoot

A field guide to wedding planning when you're not the bride *(but wish you were)*.

Dancing
BAREFOOT

© Copyright 2021, All rights reserved.

No portion of this book may be reproduced by mechanical, photographic or electronic process, nor may it be stored in a retrieval system, transmitted in any form or otherwise be copied for public use or private use without written permission of the copyright owner.

Cover design by DG Marco Álvarez
Layout by LDG Juan Manuel Serna Rosales

For more information, contact:
Fig Factor Media | www.figfactormedia.com

Printed in the United States of America

ISBN: 978-1-952779-57-2
Library of Congress Control Number: 2021908676

TABLE OF CONTENTS

Acknowledgements 6
Foreword 8
Introduction 10

Part 1: She Wasn't Supposed to be Married First 11
    The Story..12
    The Announcement..19
    The "Now What?"..21
    The Engagement 22
    The Problem 23
    The Reality: History is Against Us 26
    The Stats Don't Lie..29
    The Advice..32

Part 2: Making the Most of It (Being the best Maid of Honor on the PLANET) 35
    The "Dealing with Family" Dilemma 35
    The Feeling of Being At Odds with Nature 38
    The Mediator...45
    The Reminder..48
    The Supportive Brainstorming Process................................49
    The Scale is No One's Friend 50
    The Dress 52
    The Dreaded Bridesmaid Dresses...54
    The Engagement Party..57
    The Bridal Shower...60
    The Bachelorette Party 67
    The Rehearsal Day...74

The Big Day 77
The Primping Process..81
The Ceremony..83
The Toast..86
The Reception (AKA Party Time) 88

Part 3: Things Really Do Happen for a Reason........................91
The Wedding Aftermath 91
The Tables Will Turn 94
The Key to Finding Your Happiness 97
About the Author 98

DEDICATION

To the greatest gift my parents ever gave me, my baby sister, Trisha Pelhank. From roller-skating with our Care Bears to fighting over clothes or rocking out to NKOTB, there is no one I would have rather shared my life with. For all the good times and the hard times, I know there is nothing we can't get through if we do it together.

ACKNOWLEDGEMENTS

This book would never have happened without the love of my life, Anthony. Your unwavering support and encouragement were the push I needed to finally get this out there after 15 years! Thank you for being "smitten" all those years ago but wise enough to know when the time was right to act on it. Thank you for making my dreams come true and being an incredible father to our boys, Robby and Mick.

Life isn't always easy, and I am grateful that my parents, Mike and Terri Gilbert, showed us firsthand the importance of family. We've seen them struggle and thrive throughout their 47 years of marriage. They taught us the importance of marriage and pushing through the hard times. I am forever grateful for their unconditional love and support. Every triumph in my life is because of the foundation they gave me as a child and now as an adult.

When I married Anthony, I was also blessed with the best in-laws a girl could ask for. Thank you, Bob and Patsy DeStefano, for being another example of the importance of love and family. After 50 years of marriage, they've shown us the dedication and commitment it takes to grow together. Thank you for loving me like your own and raising the son you did.

I also need to thank the family and friends that supported me through this journey and the many since. There are far too many of you to list, but you know who you are, and you have my undying gratitude.

Thank you to Dr, Robert Kulkarni and Kay Lajeuensse for guiding me through my struggles and giving me the tools to cope with the obstacles life throws.

Thank you to Jackie, Michelle, and the team at Fig Factor Media for taking something I wrote 15 years ago and helping me transform it into this book. Thank you to my cousin, Tilly, at TillyLooks, for your mad makeup skills in my photo and to Jesus Santos at BM Photography for capturing it on film.

FOREWORD

When a loved one experiences good fortune, we are supposed to be happy for them. We are supposed to focus on them, not ourselves. But human beings don't always work like that. We can be jealous, ambivalent and angry — even towards people we are close to.

This wonderful book is about how someone makes sense of the hand life has dealt her. While on the surface it's a story about how a big sister handles her little sister getting married before she does, it's really about acceptance and growth. Here, the author explores her feelings with brutal honesty and humor while wading through all of the forces that her family, society and her own expectations place on her.

This book is a step-by-step account of the true process of how a healthy person grieves. Not by sucking it up and putting on a face. Or by explaining it away with psychobabble jargon. But by feeling sadness, anger and even humiliation but still acting in a way that is in line with who they really are. This is what the author does with authenticity and wit. She decides to be the best bridesmaid on the planet. By combining her remarkable organization and planning skills with a pragmatic (and funny!) take on the wedding planning process, she delivers a comprehensive guide that every bridesmaid should read. She embraces the role she is asked to play, and in doing so does more for herself than all of the psychotherapy in the world.

What you don't see, but I was fortunate to witness, is the author's courage to do the hard work of facing grief and deep disappointment while at the same time finding within herself the grace to give love at a time when she herself felt unlovable. I believe it is that rare quality that carried the author forward to her own happily-ever-after.

I have no doubt that she will face her future life challenges with the same tenacity and generosity of spirit. Perhaps she will continue to delight us with tales of how she cleverly slays those dragons as well.

Dr. Robert Kulkarni M.D.
Board Certified
Child & Adult Psychiatrist

INTRODUCTION

She wasn't supposed to be married first so I was (seriously) overwhelmed when my younger sister got engaged until I decided to make the most of it and be the best maid of honor on the planet because things really do happen for a reason.

This is my story.

PART 1:
SHE WASN'T SUPPOSED TO BE MARRIED FIRST

Have you ever been faced with a situation where you wanted with all your heart to be happy and supportive of someone you love, but your own emotions and issues get in the way? Yes? I thought so. It happens to the best of us and without any fault of your loved one (or you), it can be hurtful and tear apart your relationship if you let it. Recalibrating your vision goggles means letting go of what you thought was supposed to happen. Experts call this, "change management." I call it, "This sucks, what now?"

For me, the event was my younger sister's engagement and wedding. I wanted to be happy and share in all the planning and joy of the occasion, but I had never expected to be the unmarried older sister of the bride. Learning how to balance my disappointment with her joy was an emotional journey for both of us. Thus, the book you see before you.

Now, while we explore this big sister-little sister dilemma

on the following pages, know that it could easily be the best friend who was always expected to marry first and the best friend who was a confirmed bachelorette (only the latter snagged the rock on her finger first!). You see, the paradox remains the same. It's like life throws you a curve ball with a stadium full of family and friends watching from the bleachers (isn't that grand?). Through my journey, I hope your journey will be loads easier.

I should begin by telling you a little bit about myself. At the time, I was twenty-nine years old, GULP, and single. Very, VERY single. I had a promising career in finance and bought my first home at age twenty-three. At twenty-six, I bought a second car. A bright red Cabrio convertible, (you know the ones that look like Barbie cars) simply because I could. I was working on my MBA and remodeling my second home. This is where my story actually begins, in the spring of 2005. George W. Bush is president. Mariah Carey's hit song "We Belong Together" was No. 1 on the charts. And Hurricane Katrina wreaked havoc. Just like my sister's wedding announcement did for me . . .

THE STORY

I am the oldest of three. My sister, Trisha, is twenty-six and my brother, Tom, twenty-three. It is spring, 2005. Our family, including our extended family, is very close and, for the most part, all live nearby. I have fourteen aunts and uncles (eleven of which live within fifteen miles of me), and I have eighteen first cousins. There is rarely a week that goes by that I don't talk to or see at least one of them. To top that off, I grew up only a few miles from all four of my grandparents and only recently (three years ago) lost the first one, my grandpa on my dad's side. Needless to say, I've been blessed with a big loving family. It's like an Irish/German version of the Portokalos family in the movie, *My Big Fat Greek Wedding*.

There are drawbacks to that big family though. At times, they can be overwhelming and of course, there is ALWAYS drama going on. I am the oldest grandchild on my mom's side and the third oldest on my dad's side. So, growing up, I did A LOT of babysitting. I can honestly say, most of the time, I adore my family. On the other hand, there are days when I want to move far, far away. Mostly when it's assumed that I'll handle something. For example, an anniversary party for Grandma and Grandpa or a bridal shower for my cousin's fiancée, a woman I hardly know and couldn't identify with one hundred percent certainty. But the main trigger causing me to contemplate buying a one-way ticket to Cancun is when I get asked, "When are you going to find someone?"

That is the worst. Deep down, I know they mean well, but all I want to do is scream, "BEATS THE HELL OUT OF ME!"

I've been single for a very long time, and I haven't a clue why. I tried to find Mr. Right. Trust me, I tried. Friends or loved ones have said (in no particular order), "Why don't you try that internet dating thing", "I've got someone you'd really like," "You should go back to school, there are always men there,"

"Why don't you take up a sport, like golf? You're bound to meet someone that way," "How about one of those singles clubs," "You're just not trying hard enough, you should go out to bars more often," "You should do some volunteer work," "Isn't there anybody at work," and on and on and on. Guess what, I did all of that and no luck!

While most people were dating around and figuring out what their "type" was in college, I was with someone. Brett and I dated from my junior year of high school until the day before my last college final. (Yes, I totally failed that Corporate Taxation exam, but was still able to graduate!) So, my priorities were different than most of the other college kids. I figured my life was right on track and we'd end up happily ever after like I'd planned (the vision goggle thing). I had always said I wanted kids by twenty-five and, up until our breakup, it did not seem unlikely.

Then life as I knew it came to a standstill. Looking back, it wasn't his fault or my fault, it just was. We weren't meant to be, but I think you get so wrapped up in the direction things are headed or the vision you have, that you don't take time to step back and take a closer look. I didn't question if he was "the one" or if our lives were heading in the same path or if we had the same goals. Now I know, they weren't. However, that didn't help me at all during the breakup. It took me a LONG time to get over it. I spent many nights crying because I wanted my life back, or rather, the life I thought I would have or should have had. My biggest regret is that I missed the chance to be on my

PART 1: SHE WASN'T SUPPOSED TO BE MARRIED FIRST

own during those, ever so important, college years. That, in the long run, is what hurt me the most.

Since the breakup, I have been on a handful (and I do mean that literally) of dates, but no one that I have seen for more than a month. Boy, have I gone on some doozies. One first date told me I shut my TV off wrong when he picked me up. Ummm, A) My TV B) Is there really a "wrong" way to shut off a TV? C) What?!?!? Another told me about his itchy back. Spoiler alert: It was itchy because he had severe acne on his back which I heard about in detail over dinner! There was a guy who commented repeatedly on my French manicure and moaned (like, creepy 1980's porn moan) when he asked for a hug at the end of the night (yes, I showered the second I got home). There was a really cute guy from work that unbeknownst to anyone had a ton of tattoos and piercings...some in places that should not be pierced if you know what I mean. He thought buying his MOM new nipple rings was totally normal (YIKES!) I could go on, so when people say they're going through a "dry spell," I just laugh. I'm going through a "dry life." My parents and family cannot understand why it is so hard to meet someone. One year, my Mom actually bought me *Dating for Dummies and The Complete Idiot's Guide to Dating* for my birthday (umm, thanks, I think).

Back to the reason for this book. Trisha has been dating Brad for several years. He's a nice guy. A few years older than I am and I know he loves my sister. My brother, Tom, is ALWAYS with a girl. He was in a long-term relationship, very similar to what I was at his age. They dated in high school and through him going to boot camp. (He's a Marine Reservist . . .just like my ex.) However, she was, well . . .not exactly stable. It took some time for him to realize it, but he did and is now enjoying the single life.

Family get togethers have long since become uncomfortable for me, because I am always the odd (wo)man out. A few years ago, my dad surprised us all and got tickets for a Christmas concert in downtown Chicago. He rented a limo, had dinner reservations, the whole shebang. Well, he got ten tickets. Grandma, Grandpa, Mom, Dad, Trisha, Brad, Tom, Tom's girlfriend of the moment, me, and one for my date. Full panic mode hit; I couldn't go to that. I was literally sick thinking about it. I had no one to bring. When I asked him why he did that and who he expected me to take he responded with, "Come on, it's not that hard. You can find somebody." Wow. I spent a month in full depression and anxiety. Until, I convinced my mom that Tom should forgo bringing a date since he didn't have anyone serious and we should give those tickets to my Aunt and Uncle. Phew, crisis averted! That was a close one! My anxiety over being the odd man out would have prevented me from going otherwise. We ended up having a lovely evening, even if Tom and Dad fell asleep during the performance.

For a few years, I have been working with a therapist and was recently diagnosed with an anxiety disorder. So, I have been forced to work through a lot of my anxiety and face things head on. The treatment improved my life tenfold. I can't imagine facing the next few situations without the tools I gained from therapy.

PART 1: SHE WASN'T SUPPOSED TO BE MARRIED FIRST

When my ten-year high school reunion rolled around, I decided to go. Despite the fact that the only person I still talked to regularly from high school is my life-long friend, Bryan. For the months leading up to the event, I was very anxious. The week before, Bryan (who lives in another state) tells me he's not going. Somehow, I managed to go anyway. At first the football game was very lonely; it felt like everyone had a significant other. I actually left the game in tears and went to my parents' house. As I was explaining how hard it was to my mom, I could hear my therapist's voice in my head, telling me I had to tackle my fears. So, I did. I went to the bar everyone was hanging out at after the game. Guess what, I had a blast! The next morning, I was raving about what a great time I had, that I convinced Bryan to catch a flight (he's a pilot, so it was not that hard) and come in for the big party that night. Since I already had a hotel room booked, he was going to crash with me (and no, not like that. He is like a brother to me. We have literally been friends since our moms were pregnant). I picked him up at the airport, we stopped at the liquor store for a few necessities, and went straight to the reunion.

At one point, I was doing a shot with a few people, when one of the former cheerleaders came up and said, "Oh my God, Tammy is doing a shot, I don't believe it." I turned to her as the former Class President/Miss Goody Two Shoes who has since hung up her spotless slippers and said, "It's been ten @!*$ing years, grow up" and downed my shot. As the evening progressed, things get foggy. Probably because I had too many shots.

The party somehow ended up in my hotel room for a bit and the police showed up because we were too loud. Everyone, including me, found it hysterical, that they were at MY door. Considering my class president, goody goody image in high school it was quite the change. The next morning, I woke up in my hotel room with Erin, a girl I hadn't spoken to since graduation, in the other bed and the hotel room door open (not just unlocked but actually open). Bryan was supposed to be in the other bed but ended up sleeping somewhere else, so Erin stayed, and we've been close friends since. (Don't worry, Bryan was perfectly fine. I found him the next morning. He ended up passing out in someone else's room).

Despite my anxiety and frustration that I wasn't at the place I thought I would be in ten years; I renewed some friendships that weekend that have since become very important to me. Also, I realized I wasn't the only one single and childless. In fact, about half our class was single. More importantly, the ones who were married and/or had kids did not have as much fun it seemed!

Overall, the reunion was a great testament to how far I had come. Even I was surprised.

Truth #1: Instead of being worried about what my former classmates thought of me or comparing my life with theirs, I just had fun.

PART 1: SHE WASN'T SUPPOSED TO BE MARRIED FIRST

THE ANNOUNCEMENT

If you're like me, hearing that a sibling has voluntarily chosen to start a new family unit separate from yours catches you off guard and nothing you can do prepares you for it.

In my case, I was warned two weeks earlier that Brad had officially asked my dad for permission, but my mom didn't think it would be for a while. That, however, didn't do much to ease the blow. I was at home in bed on a Monday night in April around 10:30 when Trisha called to say she wanted to stop by. Suspecting something was up, I called Mom, who proceeded to tell me that she probably just wanted to tell me she knew Brad had asked Dad.

She was actually coming to show me some brochures for reception halls they had been looking at that day and to tell me they had set a date . . .six months away! He had not actually proposed or given her the ring yet, he wanted to surprise her with that, but they agreed they wanted to do this before our brother leaves in January for another deployment with the Marines.

Trying my hardest to seem happy and not in shock, I dutifully looked at the brochure. Then came THE question, "Why don't you seem happy?" I used the fact I had been asleep as an answer and was still not fully awake, because the reality was too hard to explain to myself or her.

My friend Erin responded to THE question saying she was "just shocked." Her sister is seven years younger than her and told her over the phone that she was engaged. Coincidently, her sister's engagement was just two months before Trisha's. It was Valentines' Day weekend (which happens to be around my birthday). Erin and I had planned on going out that night. Instead, we drank a bottle of wine, watched movies, and commiserated about why we are still single. It was not the most productive way to confront our single-ness or issues but that night, having an old school slumber party (with the addition of wine) worked for us.

Back to my story, after my sister left, I spent the night alternating between vomiting and sobbing on my bathroom floor. Never in my life have I felt so alone. It's not that I don't have friends or loved ones; I just don't have THE ONE. Now as a logical, strong, independent, almost thirty-something woman there are a few things I know:

1. No man can make me happy; I have to do that myself.
2. I have made a very good life for myself and haven't needed a man to support me so far.
3. There is someone out there for me; I just haven't found him yet.
4. I have great family and friends to fulfill my life. Having a mate isn't going to make my life any fuller.

Truth #2: Even knowing these things and being a logical adult (you know Logic, he is a tiny little man with a high-pitched, annoying voice) does not make the feelings of loneliness and the burning desire to find someone to share my life with go away.

THE "NOW WHAT?"

After spending the night on the bathroom floor, I debated about calling in sick to work but decided that staying home and dwelling wasn't going to help either. So, I went in and spent the morning with my office door closed so people wouldn't notice my red, puffy eyes.

I called my friend Erin in the middle of the night because she's going through the same thing, although she has over a year to prepare for it. So, I spent a good amount of time the next day chatting with her via email.

I also talked to my friend Jamey (she's the middle of three sisters and the only one married), she doesn't grasp why it would bother me so much. She tried to be supportive, but her advice was that I needed "to find a man." (Note to self: Take Jamey off the dating support call list.)

The other call I made was to my therapist. I spent my sixty-minute session that night sobbing while she sat with her arm around me. Just talking to someone made me feel better. The decision I came to that night was that I need to make sure my sister understands:

1. That my feelings have NOTHING to do with her
2. That I am happy for her and want her to be happy
3. I just need some time to get used to it
4. That the first "Poor Tammy" comment I got, would result in a justified tongue-lashing

Since I was still too emotional to talk to her, I wrote her an email. Her response was, rightfully, mixed. She was angry about my reaction (or lack of) and felt bad that this was hurting me.

Truth #3: More than anything, she needed her big sister for guidance and support just as she had come to expect all her life (you see, we all have vision goggles).

THE ENGAGEMENT

The following Saturday, I was shopping with Mom and Trisha when Brad called Mom to say he wanted us all to meet at a bar across the street from their favorite restaurant downtown Chicago. He was officially proposing at dinner that night and then we would surprise her afterwards by being there.

I was absolutely nauseous and kept thinking that this is the last place in the world I wanted to be, but I put on a happy face for one reason: I love my sister. It was tough, but she was absolutely glowing. Trisha was really happy that I was there and must have thanked me over fifteen times. Brad hugged me and called me "sis"; he was actually still shaking with nerves. My dad excused himself not long after they got there to go to the washroom, he was in there for a while and came back with red eyes. Trisha and Brad had to step out to make phone calls to Brad's parents, our grandparents, etc. It was a lovely evening, but again I felt like the odd man out surrounded by couples (Mom and Dad, Trisha and Brad, Tom and his girlfriend d'jour, Brad's brother, Scott and his girlfriend, Becky). By the time my parents dropped me off at home that night, I was exhausted from putting on a happy face and trying to ignore how truly awkward it is to be the only one single in situations like this. I spent the next day in bed recovering.

Truth #4: Ultimately, I did it. I was able to put my sister's happiness and joy above my own feelings. I did this when I realized the real problem, not the one floating on the surface that seems painfully obvious to the world at large.

THE PROBLEM

The problem was not immediately apparent. My anguish came from a place even more simple and deeper than being single. The real problem was: can I offer any "big sister guidance" when I've never been in the same situation? As girls, the older sister always does everything first. First to lose a tooth, go to school, ride a bike, start menstruating, go on a date, drive a car, go to college, etc. And younger sisters always look to their older sister for advice when it's their turn. Trisha and I are no different.

I remember about six months after I got my driver's license letting Trisha drive the car. We were vacationing in a rural area of Michigan on the way back from the store. Trisha was fourteen and didn't want to do it at first, but I convinced her it would be okay and our secret. So, I let her drive for maybe a half a mile. Like normal, I was excited to teach my little sister something new. She was excited to learn and share an adventurous secret. When I went away to college, she came to visit for a weekend with a friend and I took her to her first college party.

When I broke up with my boyfriend, she was there. She saw first-hand how hard it was and how much pain I was in. Being with Brett for almost seven years, he was part of the family, so it was painful for them as well. I think that's why it took her so long to introduce Brad to our family. She was afraid of letting herself fall too hard for him and have the same thing happen to her. Although they had been together for quite some time, it took YEARS before she finally introduced Brad to the family. Her standard response whenever asked about him was, "It's not like I'm going to marry the guy". (Yes, I did use this in my Maid of Honor toast! EVERYONE knew she had fallen hard for him!)

See, all our lives, it had been me teaching her and guiding her to new experiences (both good and bad). Now everything I had known for the twenty-seven years I'd been a big sister had been tossed out the window and it didn't feel natural!

My mom, who is also the oldest, often jokes that I was the "guinea pig." Since everything happened to me first, my parents learned what worked and didn't work with me, so they didn't make the same mistakes with my siblings. Now, when it came to a family wedding, the mistakes would be made with Trisha first.

Many of my inherent traits are stereotypical of being a first born.

Research shows that firstborns are accustomed to being the center of attention, because your parents had more time to spend with you in the early stages of life. They are also likely to be reliable, conscientious, structured, cautious, controlling, and achievers. We are often given more responsibilities and chores around the home which can lead to extra pressure and stress. We have a tendency to be Type A with a fear of failure. Stepping out of our comfort zone is not something firstborns do easily.

Middle children are usually quite the opposite. They tend to be people-pleasers, more rebellious, and peacemakers with large social circles. Middles often feel resentment to their trailblazing older siblings and attention seeking younger siblings.

Youngest children are often looked at as fun-loving, uncomplicated, manipulative, outgoing, and sometimes even self-centered. They are natural charmers and captivate attention but can feel less important as none of their accomplishments are new to their family. They are also less likely to be disciplined growing up and are not always held to the same standards as their older siblings.

My family fits these stereotypes to a T. Trisha always wants everyone to be happy and does not like confrontation. Tom on the other hand is outgoing and funny. He has a smirk that just makes you laugh or smile . . . or both.

When things happen out of order, many of those traits are unnaturally thrown out the window. It simply does not feel right. It makes us question our lives and the decisions we've made.

If you are like me, you probably didn't grow up thinking you'd be in this situation, you just assumed you'd be married first because you've done everything else first. Your vision goggles imagined that when your sister got married, you'd know the look in your father's eyes when he gave her away because you'd already seen it. You'd be able to tell her what you wish you'd gotten at your bridal shower. You probably even envisioned your children would be the flower girl and/or ring bearer at her wedding.

Truth #5: Things change and the life we think we have mapped out can quickly unravel in front of us.

THE REALITY: HISTORY IS AGAINST US

Faced with my new reality, I dug around a bit and found that I'm not ALONE! Throughout history the issue of the younger sister marrying first has continually come up, so it's nothing new.

William Shakespeare approached the subject in "The Taming of the Shrew," in which little sister, Bianca has fallen in love; however, her father has stated she cannot be married until Katherina, his older daughter, is married. The plot revolves around Bianca's three suitors and the attempts made by all, including the father, Baptista, to find a husband for Katherina.

The Bible even discusses the topic in Genesis 29:16-35 with the story of Leah and Rachel. Rachel, the younger sister was strikingly attractive and had a promising suitor in Jacob. However, their father, Laban, explained that it is customary for the older daughter to marry first. So, he pawns Leah off as the bride at the wedding ceremony.

Or take the story of "Fredrick the Great and his Friends" by L. Muhlbach written in the 1800s. In this story, Princess Ulrica is the eldest of two unmarried sisters of the king. When

PART 1: SHE WASN'T SUPPOSED TO BE MARRIED FIRST

Count Tessin, a Swedish ambassador, asks the king for the hand of younger sister, Princess Amelia, the king allows it. Stating, "Happily, we are not Jews, and our laws do not forbid the younger sister to marry first. To refuse the prince the hand of Amelia, or to offer him the hand of Ulrica, would indicate that we feared that latter might remain unsought. I think my lovely and talented daughter does not deserve to be placed in such a mortifying position, and that her hand will be eagerly sought by other royal wooers."

Even the *Addams Family* approached the subject in 1965, when, on her thirteenth wedding anniversary, Morticia tells the children how she and Gomez met. As the story goes, Gomez was promised to Ophelia (Morticia's older sister), however, he fell instantly in love with Morticia. Gomez tries to help by finding a husband for Ophelia in Cousin Itt. Although the relationship did not work out, Morticia and Gomez proceeded to marry. Throughout the series problems with Ophelia's ability to find romance reoccur.

A 2005 major motion picture addressed this issue in The Wedding Date with Debra Messing and Dermot Mulroney. Big sister, Kat Ellis, fears going dateless to the wedding of her sister. In the movie, her mother and sister take every opportunity to remind her that she is a failure because she did not marry first. In the end, Messing hires Mulroney as her date for the wedding and ends up falling in love with him (Seriously, that would ONLY happen in the movies).

In addition to the presence of these stories, there are cultural references we can refer to as well.

In a Khmer family (Khmer's make up 90% of the Cambodian population), there is a family rule that siblings MUST marry in birth order. Their belief is that if the younger sister marries first, the older sister will have a hard time finding a husband.

In the Eastern European country of Belarus, one of the oldest wedding traditions is the "order of priority." Meaning that the oldest daughter is to marry first, followed by the next in age and so on. If a younger sister marries first, it is considered a major embarrassment for the family.

As noted in "Frederick the Great and His Friends," a Jewish law stated that the younger sister may not marry before the older.

There is a Cajun tradition in which the older unmarried siblings of the bride or groom are to dance with a broom at the wedding reception, to mock their single status. Additionally, in the Cajun culture, the older siblings perform a Hog's Trough Dance. For good luck, they are to literally dance in an empty hog's trough until it breaks (Can you imagine how embarrassing that would be? No thank you!)

In French speaking Ontario, the Sock Dance ritual punishes unmarried older brothers or sisters of the bride and groom. The older sibling is called to the dance floor and asked to remove their shoes. The younger bride or groom then puts a pair of multicolored knee-high socks decorated with bells, pompoms, feathers, etc. on them. The older sibling is then expected to get up and dance ALONE while all the guests watch and cheer (There is literally, zero chance I was doing that!).

There is also an old wives' tale that created a way for an unmarried older sister to forgive the younger sister. If the elder sister dances barefoot at the wedding, she will not be destined to remain unmarried (Finally! This one works for me as I typically kick off my heels before we get to the Cha Cha Slide).

Truth #6: If all of these people before me could come to terms with their situations despite the completely embarrassing repercussions then I would certainly be just fine.

THE STATS DON'T LIE

Based on my group of friends, it seemed to me that younger sister's "jumping rank" is occurring more frequently, but I wanted to find proof that I was not the sole person in the world who felt this way. Since I am a numbers gal (A.K.A, nerd with an accounting degree) I decided to take a look at some statistics on marriage to help me put things in perspective.

Turns out my hunch was right, mainly on account of women waiting longer to marry than any other time in history. Women are now delaying marriage to complete college and start a career. In today's society, the median age for women entering into their first marriage is increasing.

By the age of thirty-five, about 74% of men and women will have married. By the age of sixty-five, 95% will. With those statistics, you can clearly see that most of us will marry at some point. In fact, the average American spends more of his or her life unmarried than married!

Despite the numbers, it does not mean more women are alone. In fact, there has been a steep incline in cohabitation. According to the U.S. Census Bureau, the number of unmarried couples living together is ten times greater in 2000 than it was in 1960. The increase from 1990 to 2010 was 138%! In total 41% of American women ages fifteen to forty-four have cohabited at some point. In the twenty-five to thirty-nine age range approximately half of American women have cohabited. The actual breakdown is:

9%	Ages 15-19
38%	Ages 20-24
49%	Ages 25-19
51%	Ages 30-34
50%	Ages 35-39
43%	Ages 40-44

Of the different sex cohabiters, 55% will get married within five years of moving in together, 40% break up within five years and 10% remain unmarried longer than five years. In actuality, 75% of cohabiters say they plan to marry their partners.[1] The majority of couples getting married today have lived together with 53% of American women having cohabited prior to their first marriage.

The cause of this may be attributable to the increase in the number of women in college; in fact, there are 72.5% of girls entering college after high school as opposed to 65.8% of boys.

With the delay of marriage, women are delaying starting families as well. In 1970, the average age of first childbirth was twenty-one. In 2018, that number had jumped to twenty-seven. The medical world considers anyone over the age of thirty-five as having an "advanced maternal age." (Seriously, couldn't there be a better name!) In 1981, only 7.6% of births were to women in this group. In 2015, that number was 25.9%! As that age continues to increase, so does the number of women needing fertility treatment. It is now said that one in ten women need assistance getting and staying pregnant. So, the stigma of infertility and "advanced maternal age" is lifting rapidly. Therefore, young women should not stress as much as they once did about fertility.

Many women, myself included, have made the decision to be a single mother if need be. Personally, there is one thing that I feel I need to do in my life: be a mother. If I find a man that I feel is worthy of me and my future child (or children) great, but on the other hand, I refuse to let the lack of a man in my life stop me from my goal. If I do not meet "the one" before I am thirty-five, then I have made the decision that I would be okay being a single mom. Fortunately, I'm not alone in this. 33% of all births are to unmarried women. Even more reassuring is the fact that for women in the thirty to thirty-four bracket, 59.5% of births were to unmarried women in 2018 and 10.6% for women forty to forty-four. So, if you are like me and are making a plan to be a single mom, if that is the way your life heads, you aren't alone.

Truth #7: There are millions of women facing the same life choices.

THE ADVICE

I wish I could say there was a big lightning bolt moment that turned things around for me, but the truth is there wasn't. Those ta-da epiphanies only really happen in cartoons. It was painful, it was hard, but I was determined to overcome my feelings and learn to recalibrate my vision goggles. Here's how I did that:

1. *Identify*

Whatever the source of your emotions, take some time to identify and address them. Write them down, say it out loud, make a list. Do what you need to find the real source of your emotions. For example, my sister's engagement was making me feel lonely and did not match what I expected for my life.

2. *Why*

Once you figure out the source of your feelings, seek to answer the WHY. Your why likely has nothing to do with your loved one. Once you realize that, you will be in a better place to communicate it to her and start a dialogue. For example, maybe you are newly divorced, and her happiness is reminding you of how you once felt.

3. *Problem*

Figure out what problem these feelings are causing or are going to cause. My problem was I did not know how to give big sister advice when I had never been a bride. Maybe your problem is that you do not have as much time as you would like to be involved in the planning and it is giving you anxiety thinking about disappointing your loved one or missing out. Be honest with yourself so you can be honest with her.

4. *Communicate*

I won't lie to you, this is the hardest part, but you absolutely MUST communicate with your loved one. You owe it to her to explain what you are feeling, why you are feeling it and what you plan to do about it. She needs to understand that it has nothing to do with her, and that you are working through it. Ask her for patience with you as you come to terms with your personal issues.

5. *Seek*

If it helps, and it did help me, seek out others with similar situations. Look for historical evidence of your "issue" in others. Do some research on the stats related to this issue. Once you realize you are not alone with this mass of emotion you are in a better position to move on. If available or possible seek out the help of a therapist. Just listening to a third party is sometimes all you need to begin to heal yourself.

Truth #8: Nobody is an expert at life. If you find someone who says otherwise, they are lying. The rest of us? We're just figuring it out as we go along, and that's exactly how I stumbled upon the path to becoming the best maid of honor on the planet.

Part 2:
MAKING THE MOST OF IT (A.K.A. BEING THE BEST MAID OF HONOR ON THE PLANET)

Navigating the upcoming nuptials goes from impossible to "we got this" when you know what to expect and what to bring to each situation. Once you make the mental leap forward, you then have to bring it on all levels. You won't be caught unaware, though, because guess what? You're going to be the best maid of honor/bridesmaid/sister/friend EVER. Read on ...

THE "DEALING WITH FAMILY" DILEMMA

Now that you have some ammo and realized that you aren't going through this alone, let's talk about dealing with family. After wading through so many emotions, I needed a *game plan* for dealing with the inevitable comments on being the unmarried older sister. Strategy time! The way I saw it there were a few options:

1. Slap each of them
2. Fly to Tahiti until the wedding was over
3. Have a smart ass comment ready
4. Ignore them
5. Just smile

Number one may land me in jail (probably not the route to take). I wouldn't want to miss this for my sister, so number two was out too. That left me with three tactical choices that I decided would need to be used at different times. I came up with a list of responses to have ready, when the situation called for it:

1. I'm really glad you pointed that out; I might have gone home and waited all night for Mr. Right to come home.
2. Yea, maybe I'll be next, but maybe you'll be the next funeral I attend.
3. My parents are starting a fund to buy me a husband, would you like to contribute?
4. I heard marriage makes you ask dumb questions and that's not really my thing.
5. What? And spoil my sex life. No Thanks.
6. I wouldn't want my parents to drop dead from sheer happiness.

PART 2: MAKING THE MOST OF IT

7. We'd really like to, but my boyfriend's wife just won't go for it.
8. Why aren't you thin (pretty, rich, handsome, smart… insert your own here)?
9. I was hoping to do something meaningful with my life.
10. Because I just love hearing this question.
11. My fiancé is awaiting parole.
12. I'm still hoping for a shot with Brad Pitt (George Clooney, Matt Damon…insert your own celebrity crush).
13. It didn't seem worth the blood test.
14. Thanks, but I already have enough laundry to do.
15. They just opened a great singles bar down the street and a husband would get in the way of that.
16. Wow, that's a great question, no one has ever asked me that before. Let me think about it.
17. My psychic says it'll be a few more years.
18. Oh, I am married, this is my husband Bob (put your arm around an imaginary date and giggle).

Truth #9: In all seriousness, there will be comments and questions. You just have to steady yourself and be prepared for them. It gets easier, to put on a smile and cuss them out in your head eventually.

THE FEELING OF BEING AT ODDS WITH NATURE

With my list in place, I figured I was ready to start embracing the upcoming nuptials. Since the wedding was going to happen whether I was on board or not, I might as well get on board and quickly. I decided that being part of the planning process would help ease me into the reality of what was happening, even if I couldn't share any real-life experience.

One evening, my sister gave me a bouquet of tulips and a lovely little book called "Bridesmaids" with a message written in it saying that she wanted me to be her Maid of Honor and that she loved and needed me. After a tearful hug, I agreed. The following weekend, we went to look at reception halls and started looking at bride magazines and websites together. One of her friends and bridesmaid, Mandy, came by and jokingly told me she found a place to rent a date and if it came down to it, she planned on renting someone for the wedding. Ummm, not a bad idea. It would help cut down on the questions and comments from family members but on the other hand, a little too much like the movie for me.

If you're like me (and most first-borns), you tend to take charge. You're usually the one "running the show." You're the organized one, the one that usually does the planning, so stepping back feels odd and unnatural. In truth, it is extremely difficult to change your patterns and actions.

For me, I've been dubbed Tammy the Party Planner by everyone. If there is an anniversary, birthday, baby shower or bridal shower, I'm the one that usually plans the majority of it.

PART 2: MAKING THE MOST OF IT

I don't mind, in fact, I enjoy it. But when it comes to planning your little sister's wedding, there is a very thin line between being helpful and being bossy.

Being a bossy big sister is undoubtedly going to lead to arguments and given your emotional state, any argument will be heated. So, keep a few things in mind. Actually, write them down and carry them with you, post them on your fridge.... whatever you do, do NOT forget them!

1. This is not your wedding.
2. You will have a wedding of your own one day.
3. Do not offer your opinion unless directly asked for it.
4. Be sensitive, this is a stressful time for her.
5. Take care of yourself, this is a stressful time for YOU.

Let's unpack these in a wee bit more detail . . .

1. **This is not your wedding.** Being the big sister, I tend to assume I know what is best, but needed to keep reminding myself that weddings should be a reflection of the bride and groom. Therefore, their tastes and interests should be incorporated (even if they are not what I would want or do).

Take the colors my sister decided on...Brown and Blue. Okay, not really my first vision when I think of pretty, but I just smiled and said, "Whatever you want." When the rest of the bridal party heard the color choice, not everyone was as quiet about their opinions. One bridesmaid would be VERY pregnant at the wedding and laughed that she would look like a UPS truck. My dad asked my opinion of the combo and I told him it wasn't my first choice, but it wasn't my wedding. Truthfully, after looking around, the combo did grow on me and it ended up looking stunning. But since I didn't tell her I hated it when she first told me, I didn't have to eat crow about it later. Your best bet during this is to lean on a friend. Complain until your heart's content, just not to your sister or another family member.

2. **You will have a wedding of your own one day.** So, by keeping your visions to yourself, you can keep them and use them for yourself. I am not saying do not offer any ideas, but if your dream is a springtime outdoor wedding with lilacs and tulips, do not insist your sister do the same when she is thinking crisp fall air and bright yellow sunflowers.

While going through the process, you will probably go through the "I'll never have a wedding of my own" phase and want to impress all your girlhood daydreams on your sister's wedding. Every little girl dreams about her wedding, I think it is something imposed on us at birth. Granted, your wedding day visions change constantly. When you were ten, you totally envisioned lace fingerless gloves or something equally ridiculous, hopefully, you have outgrown some of those ideas, but you still have your vision. When you are going through the "I'll never have a wedding of my own" phase, you will be tempted to push ALL your ideas and vision on your sister. But this is HER wedding, so her vision is what needs to come to life. Plus, you do not want to give away all your really cool, unique ideas because you won't be use them for yourself. You wouldn't want people thinking you copied her right?

Think of it this way . . . remember the scene in Friends where Rachel has just given birth and is trying to decide a name for her baby girl? Monica tells her she's already picked out a name but isn't going to tell her because she doesn't want Rachel to take it. Rachel promises not to use the name, so Monica spills and surprise, surprise, Rachel loves it and wants to name her daughter *Emma*. In the end Monica ends up "giving" her the name.

3. **Do not give your opinion unless asked . . . leave that for her future mother-in-law.** Seriously, how many times has someone, maybe your mom, given you advice when you didn't want it or ask for it? This is no different. If your sister plans on serving steak and lobster on a chicken budget, let her try it. If she asks what you think about the menu, then you can gently tell her that it might be hard and suggest something in between.

My sister, like many middle children, has trouble making decisions. More than once she said, "I wish someone would just decide for me." This may sound like an invitation to butt in, but trust me, it isn't. You need to run the other way. In the end every decision about this wedding has got to be hers (well, her and her fiancé but we all know the groom's opinion doesn't really matter too much, does it?) You can, as I did, tell her which you would choose, or your best bet is to go through the pros and cons with her. Help her make a list of pros and cons of each option. See below for an example we made when choosing the reception site:

Location A	
<u>Pro</u>	<u>Con</u>
Beautiful Room	Over the budget
Has a hotel attached	An overnight stay may be too expensive for guests
Separate cocktail area	Need to rent chair covers
Hotel has activities for kids	Half hour drive from ceremony site
Has a separate bar for after party	

After making a similar list for all the reception sites being considered, my sister discussed what was most important with her fiancé. Together they needed to decide if they were willing to forgo an attached hotel for a cheaper location or not having a separate after party bar for a closer location. These are all things that you may have a different opinion on, but again, it is her decision so just help give her the tools to make the decision and go with it.

While we're on the topic, don't take it personally if she doesn't take your suggestion or advice. She's probably getting opinions from EVERYONE (your mother, his mother, his siblings, friends, coworkers, etc.) and it has got to be a difficult position. Hopefully, she'll be able to go with her gut and choose what she likes best. Unfortunately, sometimes it's a matter of politics with her future in-laws and your parents. She may not want to use the traditional Italian favor of five Jordan Almonds, but it may be important to her future mother-in-law or fiancé and she has to pick her battles. Support her no matter what decision she makes.

Now, if you're like me and tend to be a bit sarcastic or snarky (I'm guessing you probably figured that out by now). You may tend to make comments out of anger or thinking you are being funny. Do yourself and everyone around you a favor and KEEP YOUR MOUTH SHUT! Use that friend or therapist we talked about earlier to vent to. Compile all your comments and save them for a night out with friends and a bottle of wine. You may laugh at her choice of song, thinking she was joking when she wants to use *My Heart Will Go On* for their first dance, only to find she's serious. Believe me; it won't be pretty when you realize she's not kidding. Most likely, you'll end up with a crying bride or in a screaming match with her and neither of you want that!

If you can't stand someone in her bridal party, it's better to attempt to work it out. Say her friend is total "Debbie Downer" and makes the rudest comments about everything. "That dress is ugly", "Eww, you want me to stand up with him", "I'm allergic to roses", etc. Ignore her. Try to be above it. I know it can be hard, but this person is obviously (though you may not know why) important to your sister. Respect that and don't let your sister in on your secret. The tension between you and Bridesmaid Dumbass will be multiplied by 100 for your sister. Call a temporary truce (even if it's just in your head) with the person. You don't have to be best buds; you just need to get through all the wedding events without incident. After the wedding, you'll never have to spend that much time with her again (hopefully).

4. **Be sensitive. Planning a wedding is extremely stressful according to everyone I know and what I've seen myself.** There are all kinds of emotions going on with your sister. She's happy, scared, excited, frustrated, tired, and restless. You name it, she's probably feeling it. So, try to be sensitive to her feelings. Remember the goal is to make things easier for her, like you, the big sister, have been doing all her life. Focusing your energy and time on how best to support her, will help you with the emotions you are feeling as well.

Try and get her away from wedding talk every now and then. Most of her time and thoughts will be consumed with the wedding, so it may be good for both of you to take a break from it. See a movie (without a wedding scene). Get a pedicure together. Have dinner and make a "no wedding talk" pact.

Through the process you may feel like you are playing second fiddle and you probably are, that's why it's important for both of you to take time out from everything wedding now and then.

5. **Take care of yourself!** Chances are your parents are pretty much wedding obsessed too, so take time for yourself.

Remember that you have a life that doesn't revolve around this one day. Do things for you and keep busy. Sitting at home feeling sorry for yourself because you don't have someone in your life isn't going to make it better. And unless you have a thing for pizza delivery men, pouting on your couch probably won't bring you closer to the happiness you are looking for.

Truth #10: Have fun (there's nothing holding you back, remember?). You're not tied down. You don't have anyone to answer to. You have the privilege of freedom and making your own decisions—something your sister doesn't have anymore.

THE MEDIATOR

During the wedding planning, there will probably be some arguments. Whether it's between the bride and groom, the parents, the bridesmaids, there will be some disagreements. Your job is to help mediate. My sister was hell-bent on wanting to splurge for chair covers since she did not like the chairs at the reception hall. Mom was not okay with the added "unnecessary" expense. There were words, there were tears, there were phone calls to me. It was not fun, it was not easy, but I let both of them vent. I suggested they take some time away from each other and the topic and then revisit in a few days. Surprisingly, they listened and when they discussed it again, they actually listened to the other and ended up skipping the chair covers. By the way, the reception was stunning, I think the chair covers would have distracted from the rustic look of the room anyway.

Take my friend Erin, whose younger sister Megan was planning her wedding. Megan's fiancé is Catholic. Megan and Erin are not. Megan's parents wanted the ceremony at their church. Her fiancé's mother wanted it in a Catholic Church and went so far as to say, they wouldn't recognize the marriage unless it was in the Catholic Church. Obviously, Megan's parents were pretty upset since they are paying for much of the wedding; they believe they have more of a say. Poor Erin was stuck in the middle. She had her sister calling her to complain and her mom calling her to complain. She handled it perfectly; she stayed out of it. She didn't take a *side* and tried to calm both parties down. She made suggestions that might satisfy both sets of parents, like an outdoor ceremony and a Catholic blessing at the reception and let them vent. Eventually, as with most disagreements, it worked itself out and the wedding took place at the bride's church.

The key here is not to take sides no matter who you actually agree with. Let both parties know you are not taking sides and do not let them know what your real opinion is. Offer solutions to compromise to both and try to take the emotion out of the arguments. Lean on a third party with your frustrations. In my case, my friends Erin and Jamey were invaluable during this time. My brother, Tom, also got a ton of phone calls from me, and he would just listen to me vent then make a sarcastic joke and we would laugh about whatever the argument was.

Here are a few tips to help you resolve a family argument.

1. Encourage everyone to look at it from the other point of view
2. Look for the underlying root of the issue (i.e. Is his mother allergic to roses and that's why he is opposed to them?)
3. Avoid name calling and degrading talk (i.e. "Hey, that's a stupid idea")
4. Make sure both sides are being heard and communicating openly (i.e. If she hates lilies because that's what her ex used to give her, she shouldn't be angry when his sister unknowingly suggests them for the centerpieces)
5. Brainstorm solutions until you find one both parties can live with

Truth #11: Mediating between parties, especially when emotions run high, is not easy. But it has its perks! It brings you closer to people you lean on and, when it actually works, makes you look super wise.

THE REMINDER

Being the oldest, you may be very organized, as am I. Middle or youngest, generally don't have this same trait. So, one way to be helpful is to help keep the bride organized. Just do it in a not-so-bossy way.

As an engagement gift I got my sister a wedding planning book and some magazines. Look at the magazines and/or books on your own; they will have a timeline of events to get done and checklists for the bride. You may want to keep a copy of both for yourself. If she overlooks a detail, you'll be able to remind her. Again, remember, you are not a drill sergeant (you're really more like a four-star general incognito; just sayin') and the timeline isn't set in stone. If she's a bit later than suggested ordering flowers or booking a photographer, it is not the end of the world and you don't need to reschedule the entire wedding. Simply, ask her if she's thought of anyone she'd like to talk to and offer to make the appointment and go with her.

You cannot, I repeat, CAN NOT do it for her; she has to make the decisions on her own! Your job is to remind her and be there for her. It would not be out of line for you to look around and get recommendations for her. If you have a friend that just got married, ask her which vendors she used and what she thought of their service. Your sister will appreciate the feedback and it'll save her time. At my friend Jamey's wedding, when the bridal party was let into the reception, the florist was just finishing the centerpieces. Jamey instantly noticed that there were carnations in the arrangements and flipped out. (Rightfully so, I hate carnations too!) Words were exchanged and the florist left in tears. Imagine, if she had left the decision for the flowers to her sister, the fight between them would have been epic and put a damper on the rest of the evening. Fortunately, or unfortunately, depending on whose story you hear, it was a last-minute decision by the florist to supplement the chosen flower with carnations because she felt it looked better and no family feuds were started that day.

> Truth #12: Reminder: You CAN NOT do the planning for her.

THE SUPPORTIVE BRAINSTORMING PROCESS

As I stated earlier, I truly believe a wedding should be a reflection of the couple. If you're creative and like coming up with unique ideas, like me, go for it. Use those magazines, books, or the internet to find the unique touches that will make the wedding special for your sister and future brother-in-law. Create a shared Pinterest board with her. Just remember to focus on what she likes. If you want to start a private one of ideas you like go ahead, just make sure to keep it separate and not push your vision into hers.

Mandy, one of Trisha's bridesmaids, got her the greatest engagement gift I have ever seen. It was an accordion file covered in white fabric with tabs for all the different aspects of planning a wedding (dress, favors, invites, cake, etc.). The idea is to rip out any ideas from magazines or print outs from the internet and put them in the appropriate section, once you've gotten a few, you'll probably start seeing a trend in your sister's tastes and style. If you can't find a premade special bridal version, you can easily do the same thing with a standard file from any office supply store. It won't be as pretty, but you could decorate it, if you are crafty and motivated.

Going through the file with your sister is a great way to let her know you want to be involved and you'll learn a lot about her, no matter how close you already are. Even though we dream of this day from birth, we usually do not share the details with each other until the actual planning begins. Now you'll see your sister's dreams coming to life. By now you have probably come to terms with the wedding and your feelings are either wanning or you are doing a better job of hiding them. So, enjoy it and make the most of it.

Once you have gotten an idea of what she wants, start looking on your own. Search the internet, magazines, books, talk to friends, and other brides. Come up with ideas to make your sister's wedding stand out and reflect how special and unique she is. Just don't be offended if she doesn't use the ideas.

Truth #13: Remember, you're looking for yourself as much as you are for her. By doing this you're getting involved and excited about the wedding too.

THE SCALE IS NO ONE'S FRIEND

Okay, this is a tough one. If you are at all like me, you have a few extra pounds that you could stand to lose, and you probably want to drop some before the big day. The problem is you are under a lot of stress and a crash diet just isn't healthy. So, take it slow. Try to cut back on your caloric intake, lower your carb consumption, make healthier choices, and exercise more. Whatever you do, don't be too hard on yourself. It's okay to "slip" once and awhile. That extra glass of wine or the occasional scoop of ice cream will help keep you sane.

Everyone in your family is probably dieting and cranky right now. I know I'm a REAL bitch (well, more of a bitch than normal) when I'm doing some goofy crash diet. The no carb thing was not good for me; no one wanted to be around me. My mom literally called and begged me to stop that diet because she couldn't stand to be around me.

My point is, you know your body, so be realistic. You are not going to drop twenty pounds in a month, but setting a goal of five pounds, you can probably do. You want to look and feel good at the wedding. After all, the pictures will be around FOREVER and who wants to cringe every time they see them? But you also need to do what's best for you and your body. You are a strong woman and have a lot to feel good about, so who cares if you're a "few" pounds heavier than you'd like to be? You are you and your family and friends love you just the way you are.

If your sister turns into a calorie or exercise Nazi, try to keep her tethered to reality. She will not lose 100 pounds in six months. Unless, of course she has drastic surgery, but then she'd be recovering for a few months and she has WAY too much planning to do for that. Seriously, remind her that her fiancé didn't propose to a size zero, he proposed to her just as she is, and he loves her just as she is.

Truth #14: If weight is becoming a stressor for you, the bride or anyone involved, remind them that the scale is no one's friend and to just step away . . . it's better to eat healthy and be happy than cranky, stressed and ultra skinny!

THE DRESS

Every little girl dreams about her wedding dress and has her own vision. Your sister is no different. Being the good older sister that you are, you'll want to join her in this shopping trip . . . plus, don't you want some say in the bridesmaid dress you'll be forced to wear?

Our first shopping trip was with Mom, Trisha, and me. The entire ride to the bridal shop I felt like an elephant was sitting on my chest. This was really happening; my younger sister was getting married before me. I fought back the tears and tried not to focus on my feelings. Instead, I forced myself to be present for her. Was it easy? Nope! Did I want to stay in bed and cry? You betcha! Would drinking a bottle of moscato (shoot me, I like sweet wine) alone have been more enjoyable? Oh yea! Did I go along anyway? Of course!

I let Mom and Trisha go into the dressing room together and waited outside. This is an important moment and although they wanted me there, they also needed some time alone. I can tell you, bring something along to keep you occupied, a book, magazine, your laptop, ANYTHING, because getting her in and out of dresses is a time-consuming process and you will be bored otherwise.

My mom and sister came out of the dressing room a bit teary eyed after the first dress. Actually, Trisha was shaking; she was so nervous. Eventually, the excitement went away, and frustration set in. She must have tried on fifteen dresses that first trip! There were two she liked but nothing had the "this is it" feeling. There was one dress that I loved, it was stunning on her and sparkly with a train. Seriously, there was NOTHING to not like about it, but she didn't feel the same and quickly discarded it. I tried talking her into it, but no luck. I had to remember this is her day and not push my opinions on her. While at the bridal shop I did try on about a half a dozen bridesmaid dresses, but again, none were "it." The second trip I couldn't go with, so Mom and Trisha went alone. The third trip, on Mother's Day, we all went along with her fiancé's mother and our grandmother. We still didn't find her dress but did find the bridesmaid dresses.

When she did finally find THE DRESS, I wasn't with her, but promised to go the following weekend to see it . . . something that was important for my sister. Remember, middle children tend to seek approval and have difficulty making decisions, so getting my "approval" was important to her.

The dress is such an icon and focal point of a wedding, but it is also a deeply personal choice. The most important part of the dress is really how it makes her feel! So, whatever your sister decides to wear, find something you like to focus your comments and praise on.

Truth #15: The glow of confidence will outshine (almost) any outfit!
THE DREADED BRIDESMAID DRESSES

Picking a bridesmaid dress is a difficult task! If you've ever been in a wedding (and most of us have), wearing it is often even more difficult. It is nearly impossible to find a dress that the bride likes and will flatter all the bridesmaids. As a bridesmaid, you've agreed to wear whatever the bride decides, hopefully, at a price that won't break the bank.

My suggestion is to get an idea of what she has in mind. For example, strapless, short, long, tea length, etc. Then look at the bridal magazines or internet on your own and tear out or forward anything that fits her tastes and requirements that you also like. As the sister of the bride, you're in a good spot here. Most likely, your sister will listen to your opinion more than she would her friends/other bridesmaids, so you'll be more likely to sway her to one dress versus another. Just don't get offended if it's not what you would pick to wear on your own and remember a good seamstress can make minor modifications that will make it look better but not alter the style.

Once she's made up her mind you can help do some legwork by calling around looking for the best price on the dress. Your sister won't have the time or motivation to do so, but you can and trust me, the other bridesmaids will thank you for every dollar you save them!

There are a couple things to keep in mind when shopping. First, I don't care what the dress shop says: the dresses are NOT true to size! Don't flip out if they have you get a dress a few sizes bigger than you normally wear. They wanted me to get a size eighteen, even though I normally wear a ten or twelve! I convinced them I'd lose the two inches extra in my chest in order to get in the size sixteen, which was a good thing because it would have cost an extra $90 for a size eighteen or up! Second, try to find a shop that carries a variety of sizes of the dress you want. Many shops only carry one or two of each dress and unless you're a size four, you really can't get an idea of how the dress will look on you. Honestly, this is a huge pet peeve of mine! 72%, yes, SEVENTY TWO percent, of American women are a size twelve or bigger. Why wouldn't the shops stock dresses in bigger sizes?!? The smaller girls can get in a bigger dress and have someone pull the excess fabric back to get an idea of how the dress will look, but a "bigger" girl can't do the same. I really don't get it. (Okay, okay, enough on my rant.)

Chances are you will not LOVE the bridesmaid dress. If this is the case, just go with it. You only have to wear it for one day and you've got time to find the perfect pay back dress for her to wear when it's your turn.

If you absolutely hate it, as gently as possible, explain your reason(s) to your sister. You may not be able to change her mind, but you will be the one wearing it so she should at least know your opinion. If there is no way to budge her, be creative, come up with ideas that would make the dress more comfortable for you. For example, if your issue is that you feel it's too revealing in the chest area, take a tip from my friend Jen C. She is a large chested girl and was asked to wear a low-cut halter style dress (the bride, of course, is on the flat side and doesn't understand how uncomfortable that can be.) Her solution was to have the seamstress sew in a small panel of the excess fabric to cover up some of the cleavage.

Typically, there is plenty of fabric left when they cut it off to adjust for your height. At another wedding, Trisha had detachable straps added to a strapless gown. She went without the straps for the ceremony and pictures, but knew she'd be uncomfortable at the reception and even small spaghetti straps made her feel better.

Even if you hate the dress, it doesn't mean you're destined to be miserable the entire night. There are slight adjustments that can make you more comfortable. You may want to run your suggestion by the bride first, just to be on the safe side. Typically, she will not have a problem as long as the alteration is slight and doesn't stand out from the other bridesmaids.

For those that are lucky enough to have a bride say, "Pick whatever you want," I will offer a bit of advice as well.

1. Don't go over the top. Now is not the time for YOU to be making a statement or grand entrance. This is her show not yours.
2. Clear it with her first! Show her the dress you're thinking of and ask her opinion. She'll appreciate being asked.

Try to be consistent among all the bridesmaids. If you really want a short dress, but the others are all opting for long, go long.

Truth #16: The trick is to let your individual style show without standing out or upstaging anyone, especially the bride.

THE ENGAGEMENT PARTY

Throwing an engagement party for the happy couple would be a great gesture and good for you as well. First, if you are the one throwing the party, it will show all those nosey relatives that you are okay with this and you are a great big sister. Second, it'll give you something to occupy you during the early planning stages. However, it may not be feasible due to how quick the wedding date is, schedules, and/or distance.

If you decide to throw an engagement party, it does not need to be anything big or fancy. A barbeque would be great in the spring or summer or cocktails and hors d'oeuvres would be nice too. The only key is to highlight the couple. Display pictures of the couple from birth through their engagement picture. A lovely touch would be to put their picture on the invitation. This can be done with a color photocopier or printer. If you're ambitious, make a song list to play as background music with the songs they love or ones that talk about weddings and love. If your serving cocktails, make up a menu of what you are offering and give each drink a name that relates to the couple or has a story behind it. If the groom's favorite beer is Guinness, offer the "Brad Specialty". If the bride only drinks cosmopolitans, make a special variety called "Why She Said Yes".

If your group likes to play games, have the couples do a "Pre-lyeweds" game. Before the party ask the Bride and Groom questions about each other separately, such as:

- What is his/her favorite color?
- What was his/her favorite subject in school?
- Where was your first date?
- What did he/she wear on your first date?
- What color are his/her eyes?

. . . you get the idea. Have them write the answers on separate sheets of paper and give it back to you. At the party they will be seated back to back, the "host" will ask the questions. After they answer their future spouse will hold up the answer, he/she had written. It's always good for a few laughs if they get them wrong. Another idea would be to have the guests play a trivia game and answer similar questions about the couple.

The idea of the party is to have fun and get to know each other's family and friends. In some cases, this may be the first time the parents are meeting, or you are meeting the groomsmen, so make it a light, happy time for all.

A note about gifts, some people feel they should give a gift at this type of party, others feel they'll be shelling out enough for the couple in the coming months so don't. If you decide, make sure you note on the invitation "No gifts please" or "Your presence is your gift". Often it makes everyone more comfortable. If you do not have such a comment on the invite (or even if you do) and some guests do bring gifts, put them out of sight and DO NOT have the couple open them in front of everyone. You do not want to make those that didn't bring something feel uncomfortable.

A way around this tricky gift issue entirely, is to make it a "Stock the new couple's bar" party. Simply, state on the invitation that you would like to stock their bar and ask each guest to bring a bottle of their favorite drink. This is a nice touch and something that can be as expensive or inexpensive as the guests want. It also gives the couple a great excuse to have a party when they've settled into their new home!

Be sure to remind your little sister that she needs to send out thank you notes to anyone that did bring a gift. (You might want to consider being "Miss Not So Subtle" and giving her some pretty thank you cards and heart stamps). Little things like this may slip her, overwhelmed mind, but are very important to some guests. Yes, I know some people find thank you notes outdated and unnecessary, but there are MANY people who do not and if you care enough about these people to include them in your festivities, you don't want them to be offended. Failing to send a thank you note for an engagement gift, may lead to a lesser shower and/or wedding gift. The etiquette books say you have something insane like six months or a year to send thank you cards, but I disagree, send them as soon as you can. Check that line off the growing to do list as quickly as you can!

Truth #17: The engagement party is not required and can be as casual or elaborate as the host wants.

THE BRIDAL SHOWER

Bridal (and baby) showers are really an odd thing if you think about it. The purpose is literally to give gifts to the bride-to-be. There is no other custom that says, "Hey, bring a gift and we'll give you some food and drink, maybe a favor" and send you on your way. Curious, I did some research on this too. (Yes, I know I'm a nerd!)

According to my research, the origin of the "bridal shower" is thought to go back to the 16th Century in Belgium. Legend says that the father of a would-be bride threatened to withhold her dowry if she married her true love, (a poor but generous and kind village miller). When the poor citizens of the village heard this they "showered" the bride with small gifts to replace the value of her dowry. It's a pretty great story, but still doesn't take all the weirdness out of it. On the other hand, how much fun would it be to get bombarded with all those gifts for your new home and to share a few hours with people that love you and want to celebrate this milestone in your life.

Most likely, the planning and throwing of the bridal shower is going to fall at least partially on you. This is another shot for you to do what you want, while keeping in mind this is for your sister. The bride should not be involved in the planning or hosting of the party. How much you want to share with her is entirely up to you.

If you are the Maid of Honor, or in the bridal party and the other bridesmaids are hosting the shower as well, you will need to take the lead. This can be an extremely difficult job depending on how many hosts you have, how well everyone knows each other, where they are all located and everyone's personality.

The first thing you will need to consider is how much everyone can afford. Be sure everyone is on the same page here or it will only cause more trouble down the line. Some may want to help but have circumstances in their own life that mean they just can't. Some may still be in college and have very little extra funds, saving for a home, having a baby, recently lost a job, etc. Bottom line is everyone's financial situation is different, don't polarize anyone that can't contribute monetarily.

Take my situation, I was under the impression that the other five bridesmaids were all hosting the bridal shower and we had all been communicating via email about ideas and details. The week before the invitations were to be mailed, one of the bridesmaids informed me she wasn't planning on contributing monetarily. Unfortunately, the other bridesmaids and I had misinterpreted her responses to the emails and meaning she was fully "hosting" the party with us. Although I understood she was saving for her own wedding the following year, I didn't feel it would be fair to ask the others to pitch in more as they were all going through major life changes as well, but I certainly couldn't pick up double the shares. One was due with her first baby a month before the bridal shower, one was due with her first baby two months after the wedding, and one was closing on her first condo within weeks of the wedding. After consulting with the others, we ended up leaving her name off the invitation as one of the hosts and just splitting her share among the five remaining hostesses. On a side note, this bridesmaid ended up dropping out of the wedding entirely two weeks later and our cousin, Jennifer, was asked to join in her place.

Once you've established a budget, you'll need to figure out how many people will be invited. Consult the bride for the wedding guest list. Your best bet is to ask her point blank who should be invited, however, if the shower is a surprise you will need to work through the bride and groom's mothers. You do not want to invite someone to the shower that will not be invited to the wedding.

Next, you will need to coordinate a couple of dates that work for you, the couple, the bridal party, and any other key guests, like the moms, grandma, and aunts. My suggestion is to figure out a few tentative dates that work for everyone, so you'll have more flexibility when deciding on a venue. Typically, the shower is held anywhere from eight to two weeks before the wedding.

Armed with this information you can start working out the details.

1. Location

You'll need to decide where to have the shower. Your budget, number of guests and dates will help to greatly narrow down your options. If you want the feel of a restaurant but don't have the budget, why not find a smaller venue that offers a buffet or offer a "meal" of appetizers for a late afternoon shower? Be sure to discuss how you'll handle beverages beforehand and let the wait staff know. Generally, you can specify your wishes with the restaurant, such as, if you want guests to pay for their own alcohol or that you'll pick up the tab on house wine or bottled beer only. You don't want to be unexpectedly hit with a bar tab if you didn't plan on including it. One of the main benefits of a restaurant/banquet hall for the venue is there is minimal decorating needed and minimal clean-up, which means you can enjoy the party a bit more.

2. Food and Drink

If a restaurant isn't in your budget or not the vibe you are looking for there are other options. Many subdivisions or condominiums offer a party room or clubhouse for party rental. They often supply the tables and chairs as well, so you'll just need to supply the decorations and food. Hosting the shower at someone's, usually, a member of the bridal party or a family member's, home is another option. Keep in mind you will need to rent tables and chairs if you want a seated meal, but it does give a much more intimate feeling for the occasion. With either of these there will be more decorations, setup and clean up needed, so you'll want to weigh the cost savings against the time and effort of that. Often with either of these venues many guests will ask if they can help or bring anything. Take them up on the offer if you are looking to cut costs! Most people that offer, genuinely want to help and probably have a great dish that the bride loves!

For Trisha's shower this is the route we took. The event

was held at the clubhouse in my aunt and uncle's subdivision. The hostesses bought sandwich trays, beverages, dessert, and one salad. Then we asked some of my aunts to each make an additional salad or side dish. It drastically cut the cost for us since there were 120 people on the invite list.

3. Theme/Color Scheme

For the shower, you'll probably want to choose a theme or color scheme that coordinates with the wedding colors. The internet is a great source of unique ideas. Since Trisha loves to cook, we went with a cooking theme and incorporated it into the decorations. We used her wedding colors of brown and blue for the tablecloths, plates, napkins, etc. For centerpieces, we ordered potted mums (her shower was in October), put paper chef hats around the pots and stuck wooden spoons tied with brown and blue ribbon. It was simple and turned out adorable. Plus, the mums were only $5 each! Much less expensive than hiring a florist to do the centerpieces. Another option that I have used that is inexpensive is simply balloons. Grouping three or five coordinating balloons can fill up a large space to make it feel more intimate. You can then put the balloons on a weight of anything, a chef's hat, wedding bell, you name it. You can be creative here, so have fun with it.

4. Favors

Favors can be as simple or complicated and as cheap or expensive as you want. Or, you can just eliminate them entirely.

PART 2: MAKING THE MOST OF IT

Again, the internet is a great source of unique ideas and often you can find local companies that will make them for you. Some personal favorites of mine: a single flower (just not a carnation. Did I mention that I HATE carnations? Like a serious, I will come back and haunt you if send carnations to my funeral HATE), a miniature frame, Jordan almonds in tulle, a votive in a candle holder, scented soap, candy, a decorated cookie, the list goes on and on.

I was a little over ambitious with Trisha's favors, but since everyone loved them, it was worth it. We sent a note in the invitation asking each person to mail (we did include a self-addressed stamped envelope to make it easier for guests) or email us a recipe prior to the shower. I then proceeded to type them all in a similar format along with the person's name and relation to the bride and groom. We ended up with over 120 recipes! Fortunately, my parents are in the printing business so we could have 100+ copies complete with index tab section dividers, an adorable cover, a picture of the bride and groom and spiral binding made for an insanely cheap price. My mom and I both put in countless, exhausting hours for this, but they and all of their bridal shower guests, now have a unique gift that includes old family recipes from all sides of their family. Something that they will treasure and someday pass on to their children. My point is, think long and hard before you try to take on a big task like this. We completely underestimated the amount of time it would take to do this and ended up cutting it close to finishing on time, but the end result was so worth the added stress that I would not change a thing.

5. Decorations

As with favors, your decorations can vary. I could probably write an entire book filled with just decorating ideas here, but I won't bore you with that. Check the internet, magazines, or any of the great books out there on this. Just remember to make sure the focus is on your sister and her groom. Pictures of the couple strategically placed around the room are a great way to do that. We simply made colored photocopies of some of their favorite pictures and attached them to a blue background. Then added a tag with when and where the picture was taken. Obviously, this only works if the couple has been together for some time, but could just as easily be done with pictures of the bride and groom growing up

The bridal shower is your chance to get creative, so take advantage of it. Just don't try to take it all on by yourself. If you are hosting with others, keep them involved, split up the tasks. I know it's hard sometimes for the oldest to delegate, especially, something this important but if you plan on staying somewhat sane, do it!

6. Gift

Being the big sister, you'll probably want to get her a memorable gift. I made the mistake of getting several. I just kept buying. So, to save yourself and your bank account, I've included a few great ideas I've since seen:

- Dancing lessons

- Cooking lessons
- His and Her aprons
- Books on married life
- Anything personalized with their new name
- Holiday decorations
- Several different family favorite board/party games
- Personalized stationery

As someone that is dealing with your own emotions, the best advice I have for making it through this day is to stay busy. If you are rushing around, greeting guests, serving drinks/food, or writing down who gave which gift, you have less time to focus on your feelings and emotions. You also have less opportunity to get stuck in those awkward conversations from well-meaning family members about when you will "settle down", but don't forget to review your list of responses as you get prepared to greet guests.

Truth #18: Once the shower is over treat yourself to something, a new outfit, a massage, a mani/pedi . . . or better yet do it the day before the shower as a reward to yourself for all your hard work.

THE BACHELORETTE PARTY

Most likely, your sister and future brother-in-law have already had the stripper/no stripper discussion for the bachelorette and bachelor parties. Respect their wishes! If she says she doesn't want a male dancer, don't hire one. It's not worth an angry bride (or groom), even if you think everyone else will enjoy it! The party is for her, do something she will be able to enjoy. Most of the male dancers I have seen have been pretty nasty anyway. One party, I was at, the guy actually had butt stubble! He obviously shaves his butt cheeks and hadn't in the past few days...not a good look! At another the guy went so far as to pull MY shirt to the side, place a dollar bill over my bra and take it off with his mouth! (EWWW!!) He also undid many of the girls' pants to see what type of underwear they had on. If it happened to be a thong, he thought nothing of flipping them over, pulling pants down a bit and spanking! Having some unknown man expose me to a group of friends is not exactly my idea of a good time, but hey, I won't judge you if that's your thing!

If your future brother-in-law is having a stripper and you are adamantly against it, again, **keep your mouth shut!** Your sister will be worried about the night's events already and won't need you piping in with your opinion about how wrong it is every five minutes. This is their decision, and you can't (and shouldn't) be involved. We've all heard bachelor party horror stories about what happens with the groom and a hired "stripper", but chances are most of it is urban legend and not really happening. According to my research only 1.2% of grooms (and 2.6% of brides) actually cheat during these events, so chances are pretty slim. (BTW, has anyone seen my pocket protector? My nerd-iness is really showing isn't it?)

Strippers or dancers are not a requirement for a good

bachelorette party. Actually, neither is drinking or anything tacky. Do something fun that you don't do on a regular basis to make it special. There are so many options out there. Here are a few ideas I kicked around:

- Musical or play – There are many different ones that may appeal to this situation. Some cities even have naked performances, which would be a fun twist
- Girls' weekend – How about a trip to Las Vegas or a lake house with just the girls?
- Day at the spa – Generally you can get a group rate and this way the moms can join in.
- Poker night – Act like the guys for a night
- Slumber party – This is my favorite. Go back in time to the days of sleeping bags and truth or dare. Rent movies you watched as a kid. Play games. Order Pizza and make a sundae bar.
- Bar hopping and staying at a hotel for the night – If you live near a big city, make a night of it. The hotel lets you all drink and not have to worry about driving home. Plus, there's always brunch in the morning and who doesn't love brunch?
- Do something creative – In many areas there are places that you can design your own purse or paint your own pottery (have everyone do a small salad bowl and sign a large service dish as a special surprise for the bride). There are even places to learn to knit or make jewelry.

(Do this far enough in advance that you'll have your masterpiece back for the wedding.) If your group scrapbooks, work with it, have everyone make a page or two for the bride's wedding scrapbook.

- Cooking Lessons – Find a chef to come to your home or go to their facility
- Sporting Event – Does your sister love the Cubs or the Bulls? (Yes, I am a Chicago girl). Then go to a game, contact the stadium in advance, they may be able to put a message on the monitors for her.
- Tea Party – If scheduling is a problem, why not have a small tea party or brunch? This will only take a couple hours in the early afternoon and will still allow you to celebrate with her closest friends and family.
- Pole Dancing, Strip Tease or Belly Dancing Lessons – Find a location to take a group class or hire someone to come to you. Be prepared for plenty of laughs though.

The options are endless, just make sure it's something your sister will enjoy.

Typically, these parties end up with a multitude of raunchy gifts for the bride. If your sister and you are okay with that, great. If not, suggest that each guest bring a pretty pair of panties for the bride (be sure to include her size) instead or suggest going in on a group gift. Consider a beautiful, not sleazy, negligee or bathrobe. How about a gift certificate for a couples' massage at their honeymoon site? One of my favorite bachelorette party gifts to give is bath products with a name like "sensual" or "romance." Candles and massage oils are always good gifts that aren't raunchy. If you go the raunchy route, try to keep in mind who she'll be opening these gifts in front of at the party. Would you really want to open up a pair of edible undies or a book on sex positions in front of Grandma? Probably not.

Mandy (the same bridesmaid that gave her the great planning tool as an engagement gift) ordered Trisha an adorable white tank top with pink crystals that spelled "Bachelorette." It was perfect. I went with a pair of silky shorts and a tank top pajama set. Something I knew she would actually wear long after the honeymoon. I also added a special wedding day emergency kit (more on that later) and a cute "Newlywed" bag for the honeymoon.

Normally, the bride-to-be wears some cheesy form of a veil at these things. I've seen all kinds of them, from ones with penises or condoms attached to homemade ones that weren't even cut straight. The easiest thing, and what I did, is to get an inexpensive one from the party store and embellish it on your own. I added simple clear crystals with a hot glue to the tulle and then added some sparkle and flowers to the headband portion. It dressed up the veil a bit and ended up being really pretty.

Another common thing is the "suck for a buck" shirt. Basically, the bride sells some type of candy for a dollar . . . it's actually a great way to fund those shots you'll probably end up doing if you are out on the town. It can be done a zillion different ways. I've seen lifesavers attached to a shirt . . . that would have been a bit too awkward in my opinion. For Trisha, I decorated a canvas bag with feathers and rhinestones and filled it with suckers and a sign saying, "Suck for a Buck." My favorite was a bouquet made from suckers. You can buy a handheld corsage base at any craft store. It is typically filled with foam or you can add your own. Then simply push the ends of the sucker in it and embellish it as much or as little as you want.

Remember that you don't have to foot the entire bill for this. The other bridesmaids should be willing to help you out. If you are going to something like a play or taking a lesson, it's okay to ask the guests to pay for their own ticket. Just be sure to let guests know up front that they will be responsible for paying their own portion, approximately how much it will be and when/how to get you the money. If you are having the event at your home or someone else's you can ask guests to bring a dish or a drink to share. Just don't ask the bride to bring or pay for anything and remember to have fun. This is supposed to be a way to let off some steam and stress from the past few months of planning right before the big day.

As tempting as it may be to drink away your feelings at this type of party, try to avoid it. Someone needs to be in charge of making sure everyone gets home safely. If you are lucky enough to have someone else be a designated driver (perhaps those pregnant bridesmaids), then kick back and have fun! Word of warning though, do not get to the emotional this-is-so-unfair state. You will end up saying something you will regret later and causing yourself more trouble. Save that night for an evening with your girlfriends.

You may also need to do some self-talk prep work in advance if Bridesmaid "Pain In The Ass" is going to be there. She'll likely be more annoying when she's drinking and you'll have a harder time keeping your yap shut. Prep yourself beforehand for this, enlist another guest to help get you away from her if you get stuck. Having a comeback ready is always helpful! My personal favorite response to dumb comments is "You're pretty." Imagine it . . .

Bridesmaid P.I.T.A: "Did you see so-and-so's outfit? It's totally tacky."

You: "You're pretty."

Bridesmaid P.I.T.A.: "Ummmm, thank you."

And scene.

Really, you are thinking "you are pretty dumb," "you are pretty petty," "you are pretty much the biggest a-hole I've ever met" . . . but she is too dumb, petty, and too much of an a-hole to realize you are actually insulting her so there's no comeback. It works EVERY time! Trust me. (Seriously, I use this ALL the time!)

Truth #19: Repeat after me . . . "You're Pretty!"

THE REHEARSAL DAY

You will likely spend at least part of the day with your sister, so you will want to plan ahead and take the day off work if necessary and/or possible. Whether it's for mani/pedis or a more formal bridesmaid luncheon, your sister will be going through an array of emotions and she'll need you there.

We had a simple lunch at a local tearoom with the bridesmaids, our mother, grandmother, and aunt (Trisha's Godmother) followed by manis and pedis at a local salon. The goal was to be relaxed and celebrate it together. Some brides may opt to do nothing that day and spend the day alone with their thoughts, others may be too busy with last minute preparations. If your sister is in the latter group and has last minute errands to do, try and take the stress off her by helping her in any way you can. In my case, I had taken the Thursday and Friday before her Saturday wedding off, so we ran all the errands needed on Thursday. This left her able to relax and enjoy the day Friday.

The evening before there will likely be a dry run of the ceremony followed by a dinner for the bridal party and any out-of-town guests. Don't be late for rehearsal! This is your ONE and ONLY chance to practice for the big show. Be sure to pay attention to the directions, your sister may not remember much, and you'll need to be able to prompt her if necessary. During the rehearsal, you will practice everything from walking in, to the reading and processing out.

A couple things to remember:
- If there are children in the ceremony, they generally go in right before the Maid of Honor (who goes right before the Bride and her father), so if you are in the Maid of Honor position, you'll need to be the one to tell them when to go. Make sure you remind them to walk slowly and smile. For Trisha's wedding, at

rehearsal the flower girl and ring bearer kept going too fast despite all our efforts. When the big day came, I reminded them again to walk "really slowly". It worked a little too well and they went at a snails' pace. Obviously, I had to time my entrance based on theirs, so I went a bit early. The point is, pay attention, just in case you need to improvise.

- All this talk about walking slowly applies to you too. Obviously, you won't want to look like a snail, but make a point of consciously telling yourself to slow down. The quicker you go, the quicker your sister will enter, and you'll want to remember this moment for the rest of your life. Savior it and set the pace for her big entrance.
- Pay attention to where the other bridesmaids are supposed to be, just in case one of them forget as well.
- Pubes not boobs. When carrying a bouquet it should be held low not high. My cousin (and the most amazing makeup artist ever), Elizabeth's, easy reminder to all bridal parties is hold your bouquet to cover your pubes not your boobs!
- Smile! Whatever you do, smile! You may not notice at the time, but there will be a camera and possibly a video camera on you at the ceremony. When we saw pictures from Trisha's big day, we noticed our cousin Jen didn't smile once. She looked miserable, when we asked her later, she said she was concentrating on not tripping and forgot. We still laugh about it today! So, make a point of reminding yourself to smile.

After the ceremony rehearsal, it's party time. You'll probably go somewhere for dinner and drinks (yes!!!). At dinner, the bride and groom typically give the bridal party gifts and do a toast thanking everyone for sharing the day with them. In some cases, the floor will be opened for everyone to toast the couple or share a story. If this happens, you are not obligated to speak, after all, you are giving a toast at the main event. However, if you choose to join, be sure it is complementary to both the bride and groom. See "The Toast" for more hints on this.

As tempting as it may be, be sure you don't drink too much. You cannot risk a hangover for the following day! Also, keep an eye on your sister and the rest of the bridal party for the same thing. You'll also want to make sure it is not a late night. EVERYONE needs their beauty sleep, including you!

If you are spending the night with your sister, as I did, you'll want to get her settled as early as possible, because the later she is up, the later you'll be up! Then again, it is a great opportunity to share those late-night giggles like you did as children. Trisha and I always shared a bedroom growing up and there were countless nights we'd be up talking and eventually giggling about something.

Truth #20: The night before her wedding we did the same thing…it made us both feel better to realize that no matter what, some things never change.

THE BIG DAY

Okay, the day is here…everything from the past few months has led up to this one single day. Hopefully, you have followed my advice and gotten a good night's sleep because, girlfriend, you will need it!

Be prepared! Being the organized one and the one that generally takes care of everyone, you will feel more at ease and content if you are prepared. To be on the safe side, make up a tote bag to carry with you to the ceremony and reception. As mentioned earlier, I made an emergency kit up for my sister as a gift, in a cute "just married" bag. I also made a version for myself as well. Here's a list of items that should cover almost any minor crisis:

- Aspirin (or any pain reliever)
- Band aids
- Bottle of water
- Clear nail polish
- Corsage pins (these suckers break or get lost all the time)
- Eye drops
- Extra cash
- Extra earring backs
- Bobby Pins
- Ponytail holder/Rubber band
- Hand wipes
- Hand Sanitizer

- Hem tape
- Matches/Lighter
- Mini Sewing Kit
- Safety Pins (various sizes)
- Scotch tape
- Chalk (sounds strange, but it can cover a smudge on the Bride's dress if needed)
- Sedatives (Don't ask, it can happen)
- Scissors
- Smelling salts
- Static Cling spray
- Spot Remover
- Pens/Notebook
- Loose Powder (No one wants a shiny face in pictures)
- Straws (No messing up lipstick!)
- Tissue
- Coloring books & crayons (to settle any children guests)
- Tweezers
- Wrinkle out spray
- Mints/Spray
- Brush and Comb (for the guys)
- Dental Floss
- Mouthwash
- Antacid
- Toothpicks
- Extra pantyhose (if the bridal party is wearing them)

PART 2: MAKING THE MOST OF IT

- Hair Spray
- Linen Handkerchief
- Nail File
- Small Mirror
- Deodorant
- Tampons/Pads
- Flats or flip flops
- Snacks (Cereal bars, nuts, etc.)
- Super Glue (works for nails, broken shoes, decorations, etc.)
- Benadryl (if someone has allergies, they will thank you)
- Sunblock
- Extra phone charger
- Portable charger

Some of this may sound crazy now but let me offer you some insight. When my mom was the Maid of Honor at her sister's wedding, she fainted at the altar! Full on, head hit the floor, fainted! Fortunately, many of the guests were firemen/paramedics and someone had smelling salts, but it was super embarrassing for her! I've been to two weddings (yes two separate weddings!) that the buttons on bridesmaids' halter dresses popped off. One was lucky enough to catch her top, the other bridesmaid gave anyone in view a great show! Safety pins saved the day in both cases and the bridesmaids could continue to enjoy the evening (even if they were red faced from embarrassment all night).

Brides sometimes "forget" to eat on the day of the wedding, so having a few snacks is key. (Side note, I seriously think I have more in common with a serial killer than someone who forgets to eat, but I suppose it could happen...yes I'm rolling my eyes.) Children get bored quickly and easily, so having something to occupy them will make you the hero to anyone seated near them!

My dress gave me some SERIOUS cleavage (imagine, two hot air balloons colliding mid-air) and I was very uncomfortable during the ceremony. I didn't have any hem tape, but a beloved family member noticed my awkwardness and happened to have upholstery tape in her car (she will forever be my hero for that!). A little tape here and there, and I was able to gain some modesty back, which made the rest of the day much more comfortable.

Truth #21: The big takeaway: make sure your emergency supplies are in an easy to reach place and nearby all day.

THE PRIMPING PROCESS

Hopefully, you have appointments for your hair and makeup at some point during the day. Be on time, even early to these. If you have a group or all of the bridal party is going to one salon, be flexible. Some bridesmaids may not like how their hair or makeup turn out. You'll want to leave your sister out of it and try to solve as much of the problem as possible. That may mean reinforcing (okay, lying) to a bridesmaid that she does actually look good or that sometimes different is a good thing. It is okay for your hair or make up to look different that you normally wear it on a special occasion, actually, now is the time to try something new. It may also mean pulling out your mediator hat and trying to get a stylist to understand how the bridesmaid wants it. Either way, be flexible.

I was fortunate, I loved how my hair and makeup turned out…however, one of the girls was very upset about her hair. So much that when she left the salon, she went straight to her normal stylist and had it redone. Although there wasn't anything I could do to intervene the day of, a few weeks later (at my next visit to the salon) I mentioned it and they graciously told me to have her come back for a refund.

Try to best to keep *everyone* to a schedule. It may be helpful to pull together a timeline for the day in advance. Professional event planners do it for a reason! They call it a "run of show". It keeps all the "performers" (let's be honest, weddings are pretty much a big production anyway) in line so they know where and when they need to report for duty.

The primping portion will, I guarantee, go by in a whirlwind, so try to take a lot of pictures and enjoy it! It may be a good idea to bring food and drinks to the salon if possible. Our salon was wonderful and not only agreed to let us bring snacks and mimosas, they supplied them for us! They went so far as to make some of the recipes from the bridal shower cookbook (I gave them copies when I was in a few weeks before the wedding.) One of the groomsmen's mother and sister worked at the salon that my family had been going to for years. So, this was a sweet extra touch. In addition, we had sandwich trays at both my parents' house for the girls and my condo (where the groom and his groomsmen were getting ready). You won't want to eat too much, but you do need to eat something!

Today's the day where you have to play problem solver. Do anything and everything to leave your sister out of any issues or problems that come up. She'll have too much on her mind and any minor glitch could throw off her entire mood. At rehearsal, one of Trisha's bridesmaids was sick but we figured she'd be just fine. Well, as we were heading to the salon, Jen called me to say she'd spent the night in the ER and was on two hours of sleep. Turns out she had a nasty flu bug and was dehydrated. I give my sister credit, she was very calm, I don't know that I would have been in her position. We decided Jen should stay home and get some sleep. Then I called the other bridesmaids and rearranged their salon appointment times so she could take the latest possible one. In the long run, Jen was so sick she couldn't even make the ceremony. We just improvised and had one girl walk with two groomsmen. Trisha was disappointed that one of her closest friends wasn't there, but she didn't let it ruin her day. In this situation, there wasn't much I needed to do, but there are many stories that don't turn out that way. In some cases, you may need to help rearrange seating for unexpected guests or improvise on fixes for wardrobe malfunctions. Just be ready with a solution and keep the bride out of it unless absolutely necessary.

At some point, the father of the bride usually gets a "first look". As tempting as it may be to hang around and enjoy that special, magical moment, let them have it alone. Give your dad some time to absorb the lifetime he has spent playing her leading man and take in how beautiful she looks before he has to hand her off to her groom.

Truth #22: You will have your own moment with him someday too.

THE CEREMONY

Waiting at the church for the ceremony to start is extremely nerve wracking. Actually, I would classify it as torture. While you are allowed to sneak out and talk to the guests, your sister is confined to one room and she is probably pacing. Distract her, if possible, and only allow a few people (other than the bridal party) in with her. You don't want all your distant relatives in there making her either emotional or more nervous! You may need to play bouncer at the door. For those persistent guests that insist on seeing her, but she doesn't really want to see, try "She's in the washroom" or "She's having a heart to heart with her grandma", that should deter them.

The actual ceremony will go by quickly, I know Trisha's certainly did. Remember to smile, you never know when your picture is being taken. Also, if you are the maid of honor, it is your duty to straighten the bride's train and hold her bouquet at the appropriate times. I don't actually remember much of her ceremony, but there is one second that stands out in my mind. Seeing her at the opposite end of the aisle with my dad. It was amazing. She looked like an absolute angel; I don't know if I've ever seen a more beautiful sight. In that flash of one second, I saw our whole lives together, me doting on her as a baby, playing dress up as little girls, fighting as teenagers. I will never forget that one second. You will want a stash of Kleenex somewhere handy (your cleavage or hidden in your hand with the bouquet) and be ready to hand one to your sister if necessary. Sneak a peek at your new brother-in-law too, the look of awe and happiness is something you will never want to forget. Just a tip, try NOT to look at your mom and/or dad…you will cry and once you start it is much harder to stop…trust me.

After the ceremony, you may need to participate in a receiving line. My only recommendation is to remember some of your comebacks from earlier and be ready to drop them as needed. There is always that one person, Mr. or Ms. Talk-Your-Ear-Off, that ties up the line by wanting to carry on a long conversation with someone in the bridal party. Since this line needs to move before you get to the good part (aka, the open bar), gently interrupt and pull over another guest while saying something like "so and so has to leave but wants to say hi first." In the meantime, you'll need to make small talk as necessary, and there will likely be hugs and kisses here, so remember breath mints and hand sanitizer for after. Also, air kisses will save your well applied lipstick. Whatever you do, DO NOT forget your comeback list. This is when you will likely get hit with the most obnoxious questions. It's perfectly fine to sneak out of line to avoid Great Aunt Mind-Your-Own-Business when you see her coming up in the line.

You will also have to participate in picture taking. I am completely unphotogenic (like an awkward 1980's class picture style). Be sure to smile as naturally as possible. I cannot for whatever reason smile well on command. It looks and feels ridiculous but try out different smiles in front of a mirror in advance. It will make you more comfortable and maybe you'll end up liking some of the pictures. There are likely several group shots your sister and new brother-in-law would like taken. If possible, review that list with them ahead of time, so you can help make sure nothing is left out and speed things along (remember, the bar is waiting!). Unfortunately, we didn't do this and missed out on several shots that would have been nice to have.

Truth #23: Don't forget to take a moment and take in the church, the guests, the beauty of two people committing to spend eternity together.

THE TOAST

Check with the bride several weeks before the wedding to see if you will be expected to give a toast, regardless of whether you are the maid of honor or not. For some people, the pure thought of speaking in public brings on sheer panic. Fortunately, I am not in that camp. If you are, prepare your toast early and rehearse it repeatedly for the week leading up to the wedding. Practice it in the car, before bed, run through it in your head while brushing your teeth. The more comfortable you are with what you are saying, the more confident you appear when public speaking.

Deciding on what to say is probably a point of stress as well. Again, there are books and websites that can offer great tips. You can share a funny story about the couple, or a story about your sister growing up or you can simply recite a poem. Your toast can be humorous, sentimental, serious, or whatever combination works for you, just make sure it comes from the heart.

You'll also want to be sure to address both your sister and new brother-in-law. At a wedding I attended, the best man stood up to tell the bride how lucky she was to be married to his best friend…and he said nothing about the groom being lucky to have her. It came across really bad and gave the impression that he did not like the bride or thought the bride was not good enough for his friend. To this day we still jokingly refer to the groom as "Saint XXX" (No, I am not sharing who it was) because of the way his best man portrayed him in the toast.

Also, don't insult or offend anyone. At another wedding, the best man literally insulted the bride, mother-of-the-bride and her family (the word "bridezilla" was used, I kid you not!). Then proceeded to tell jokes about the groom's past dating life. The entire guest list sat there in shock. Not a good way to start off the evening or a marriage for that matter. It was probably all of the excess shots before it was toast time that set him off, so do yourself a favor and hold off just a little bit longer before putting on your much deserved drinking hat.

There are two maid of honor toasts that really stand out in my mind. Both were from friends of the bride. The first, reviewed a list the bride had made when she was in college of what she did or did not want in a future husband, including no one from Notre Dame (she is a University of Illinois alum), and no lawyers…her husband is a graduate of Notre Dame's law school. The other listed things she'd learned during her lifelong friendship with the bride (with an entire bottle of champagne tucked under her arm the whole time), such as, you can never have too many $7 shirts, buckets of beers are always a good idea, and when you find the perfect guy hang on to him. Both of these women went the humor route, but both addressed the groom as well. They were perfect. My favorite best man toast, worked with the DJ in advance to incorporate a few clips of embarrassing songs the groom had on his iPod (yes, it was a while ago).

You will also want to know how many other people will be toasting, so you can alter the length accordingly. There is nothing worse than sitting through several long boring toasts while your dinner is sitting in front of you getting colder by the second.

If your father or another family member is not toasting, be sure to welcome your new brother-in-law to the family. No matter what you decide to say, you will want to keep some Kleenex available just in case you get emotional. It also helps to have it written out (or better yet, bullet point the main talking points), that way if you get stage fright or overly emotional, you have something to refer to.

Some final points on public speaking:
1. Speak slowly…when your nerves kick in people tend to speak more quickly than they realize

2. Don't read it…we've all seen people read their entire speech and it isn't pretty. If you've practiced you shouldn't need to refer to your notes, unless it's a quick glance.
3. Speak loudly and clearly…you will probably have a microphone, but that doesn't mean you can whisper it and you don't want people around the room whispering, "What is she saying?"
4. Smile…don't look like you are giving someone's eulogy. This is a happy occasion, act like it.

THE RECEPTION (AKA PARTY TIME)

This is it, the moment you have been waiting for! The wedding ceremony is over, the formal pictures are taken, your toast is complete, all you must do now, is enjoy yourself! Have a few cocktails, dance, visit with guests, flirt with the grooms' friends. Just don't get to the drunk idiot phase. Do that next week without so many prying eyes. There is a fine line between fun and obnoxious, please do your best not to cross it. Try alternating alcohol with a glass of water to slow you down. Ask a friend to keep an eye on you and cut you off if necessary. Making a scene at your sister's wedding will go down in the family history books and no one wants that story shared at Thanksgiving dinner tables yet to come.

I hate to be the bearer of bad news, but there are still a few tasks you need to be available for during the reception (fortunately, you should be able to handle these with a slight buzz).

PART 2: MAKING THE MOST OF IT

1. **The bustle.** Have you seen a wedding dress lately? They are huge and if there is a train, it likely needs to be bustled. The seamstress will have shown the bride how to do this, but she can't do it while wearing the dress, which means it's up to you. Take your time and listen to the instructions (better yet, try to go to that final fitting to learn yourself). It will take a few minutes but enjoy the quiet time.
2. **Dancing.** You will be asked to dance with the bridal party. If the best man is a total loser, hold your breath and make the best of it. You don't have to make out with the guy (in fact, I highly recommend you don't), but smile. It's only one song you will get through this. If possible, try to dance with your brother-in-law at some point, he's a member of the family now, this is a good start to building a relationship with him.
3. **The thing no one warns you about…potty time.** At some point, the bride will need to use the washroom. With all the layers of gown, this is nearly impossible to do without help or making a mess. Offer to go with her and hold her gown up while she goes. Is it awkward? You betcha, but completely and utterly appreciated by the bride.
4. **Take a minute to absorb the moment.** Find a quiet corner and stand back and just watch, enjoy the happiness and love in the room. Take in the décor and beauty. Give yourself a mental snapshot of this day, you

will want to remember all your hard work and how far you have come in the process. You may still be feeling vulnerable and lonely, but as long as you have made it to this day without transferring those feelings to your sister, you've done something spectacular and need to be proud of that.

5. **Dance Barefoot.** Yes, you read that right, girlfriend! Follow that old wives tale and dance barefoot! Who knows, maybe it will bring you good luck. No one needs to know why you are barefoot, it'll be our secret. Besides, you have earned it! This has been a long emotional road, take the moment to kick off the heels, relax, and enjoy it.

Part 3:
THINGS REALLY DO HAPPEN FOR A REASON

THE WEDDING AFTERMATH

Here's the thing about life, you just never know where it will lead you.

A few days after Trisha and Brad got home from their honeymoon, a group of us went out for drinks. One of Brad's best friends and groomsmen, Anthony, asked me out. He had caught the stomach bug from the bridesmaid he was supposed to stand up with and missed much of the reception. So, although I did end up dancing with his father at the wedding, I didn't spend much time with him that day.

Brad and Trisha had been trying to get us together for years, but it never went anywhere. The first time we met, Anthony told Brad he was, and I quote, "smitten" with me. (Seriously, who under the age of seventy says smitten?!?!) We had hung out quite a bit and there had been flirting but nothing more. I had all but given up any hope of anything more coming from it. In fact, earlier that night, our friend Jen C. had said that he needed to "sh** or get off the pot". (Her face when I told her he had asked me out a few hours later was priceless!)

Our first date was the day before Thanksgiving that year. A month later, I gave him a key to my condo and we bought a new couch together. Apparently, my ultra-girly single style needed to change a bit. Yup, after dating for six weeks we went "halvies" (his wording) on a new couch. I "re-met" his family on Christmas night. Bringing a bottle of Asti for his mom (her favorite) and a bag of ice for his dad (he's always concerned with having enough ice at every event, so it's a long running family joke).

My dreaded 30th birthday was three months after the wedding. My family had planned a surprise party for me, complete with Tom's special "French Martinis." Towards the end of the party, they had me open gifts. At one point, Anthony leaned over and said, "We're going to Vegas, baby," then a limo driver walked in and ushered Trisha, Brad, Anthony, and me out to the car! It was a magical and memorable weekend for all of us. During one taxi ride, Anthony and I were jokingly bickering, and the driver asked, "How long have you two been married?" For some reason we found it hilarious and comforting that a random taxi driver thought we were naturally a couple.

Two months after that, Anthony officially moved in. Our relationship just felt natural. We were both shocked how easily we transitioned to living together, there was no fighting or arguments about where to put things or splitting household chores, it all just fell into place.

PART 3: THINGS REALLY DO HAPPEN FOR A REASON

Three weeks before Trisha and Brad's first anniversary, our family received the biggest, most challenging blow of our lives. Our brother, Tom, was killed in action while serving the Marine Corps in Al Anbar, Iraq. The news was devastating. Tom was always such a shining light in our lives. His spirit filled every room he entered, full of joy, smiles, laughter, and hugs.

The outpouring of love and support we received from our family and community was overwhelming and awe inspiring. Two of our uncles, (Mom's brother, Dave and Dad's brother, Dan) made it to my parents' house within minutes of us calling and didn't leave our sides for weeks. They literally took turns sleeping on the couch so one of them was always there when we needed it. Additionally, Anthony, Brad, Trisha and I, all moved into our parent's house so we could be close in those first weeks. Anthony didn't leave my side. Brad didn't leave Trisha's. With their support, Trisha and I together held up our parents, literally. At the cemetery, Trisha and I sat on either side of our parents, holding them and giving them strength while Brad and Anthony sat on our other side holding us.

Somehow, mercifully, we survived. There were (and still are) days when it seemed impossible, but we made it through together.

Truth #24: How someone copes in the face of tragedy can be a true testimony to love and Anthony gave me the strength to be strong for my parents, I can think of no better way to show me his love then allowing me to grieve as he did.

THE TABLES WILL TURN

Out of this great tragedy came a slant of light. In May 2007, we were invited to a Gold Star Family event in Washington DC. (Gold Star's are issued when military is killed in action, thus we instantly became a "Gold Star Family" when Tom died). Being a history major in college, Anthony loved EVERYTHING about the trip. We had tours of all the hot spots even a private tour of the White House and Rose Garden. Unbeknownst to me, Anthony had asked my dad for permission to marry me a few weeks earlier and had even shown the ring to my sister. So, at every possible photo opportunity, my parents, Trisha, and Brad would walk away a bit to give Anthony room to do his thing. Did he propose in THE Rose Garden? In front of THE Oval Office? Any of the amazing historical monuments? Nope! He waited until the Wednesday after we got home.

Trisha and I met with someone about a website for the foundation we'd started in Tom's memory that evening after work. On the way home from the meeting, I was complaining that he hadn't proposed and maybe he wasn't going to. It had been over a year and I wasn't getting any younger. Trisha knew what was going to happen, so she just let me vent (while trying not to laugh). When I got home, I noticed immediately the condo was super cold. I found him, in the bedroom, with a ton of candles lit, standing in a suit. He had a beautiful speech, got down on one knee and proposed! It was incredible! It was everything I had dreamed. After my inevitable YES, he quickly changed out of his suit while I started making Facetime calls to our immediate family and close friends with the news. P.S., the condo was cold, because he cranked the air conditioning to combat his nervous sweating.

We had another Gold Star event in downtown Chicago the following Saturday. I was photographed for one of the major newspapers hugging the then Mayor Daley's wife, my brand-new engagement ring was in prominent view, so there was no need to tell much of our extended family. They all saw the picture and called with excited congratulations.

We were married on March 15, 2008, surrounded by 400 of our closest friends and family (He's Italian, I'm Irish...what can I say, we have ALOT of family). Trisha was my matron of honor and Brad was the best man. My two new sisters (Anthony's sisters, Dawn and Deanna), Jamey, Erin and the one girl we thought Tom would have ended up with, Lori, were all by my side that day.

Even though Tom was not with us, we set a place for him at the head table with his uniform on the chair. His best friend and fellow Marine, Andrew, walked my mom down the aisle. We served Tom's special "French Martinis" during the cocktail hour. If you had asked me two years prior to imagine this milestone of my life without Tom there, I would have said it was impossible. But just like we got through the initial shock of his death together, we got through this by making sure his memory and presence were all around us and leaning on each other. It breaks my heart that I don't have a picture of Tom and me on my wedding day, but I know he was there and smiling just as much as he was at Trisha's wedding. Fortunately, since Anthony and Brad were friends long before we started dating, Tom and Anthony had gotten to know each other pretty well and Tom was thrilled when we started dating.

Everything I had learned going through my sister's wedding was helpful in making the day all I had dreamed. In fact, remember that wedding dress I fell in love with, but my sister didn't? Well, it was still available when we went shopping for me, so my search was over before we even started! The wonderful people that took such great care of my sister's bridal party at the salon are now my in-laws. All that time looking at ideas and making suggestions for Trisha, meant I already knew what was out there. From favors, to flowers, to bridesmaid dress styles, everything was just a bit easier because we had done it before. This time though, I wasn't the guinea pig and figured out how to budget in chair covers much to my sister's dismay.

In the seconds before we were introduced as Mr. and Mrs. DeStefano at our reception, I was able to look around the reception hall at all the people we loved most and then at my new husband and took a deep, cleansing breath.

Truth #25: For all the anxiety and loneliness, I had felt when this journey started, I did not have any of it on MY wedding day. I felt calm, happy, and loved.

THE KEY TO FINDING YOUR HAPPINESS WHEN EVERYONE AROUND SEEMS TO BE LIVING THEIR BEST LIFE

At the time of my sister's engagement, I was in a bad space emotionally. I was lonely, I was jealous and resentful, I was even angry, but going through the planning of Trisha's wedding allowed me to work through my issues. Ultimately, it got me to a healthier head space, one that was open and ready for the relationship I'd been wanting for so long. I truly believe that those hard times are sometimes put on your path in life so that you are forced to learn and grow.

My life now would not be what it is if I had not gone through what I perceived as the horror of my younger sister getting married before me. Nor would it be the same if I hadn't learned to lean on Anthony when we dealt with the grief of losing Tom.

If you're struggling with your own emotions, as I was, take your time to be miserable, have that night, day, week whatever you need. Then get up, dust yourself off and have faith. Immerse yourself in the happiness of the upcoming nuptials. You may just find yourself in the process and rekindle the bond with your loved one. Whatever you do, remember good things are just around the corner.

Truth #26: Dancing barefoot may help too!

ABOUT THE AUTHOR

Tammy DeStefano is a life-long resident of a Chicago suburb. Although her degree and professional background are in accounting, she has always dreamed of authoring a book. When not working or writing, you can find her reading, gardening, or carpooling her sons, Robby and Mick. Together with her husband, Anthony, they love to spend time at the family lake house in Michigan and volunteering for the organization they started in honor of her brother, Sgt. Tommy's Kids.

www.ingramcontent.com/pod-product-compliance
Lightning Source LLC
Chambersburg PA
CBHW070855050426
42453CB00012B/2222